Daddy and Me

A photo story of Arthur Ashe
and his daughter, Camera

PHOTOGRAPHS AND WORDS BY JEANNE MOUTOUSSAMY-ASHE

Alfred A. Knopf · New York

Acknowledgments

I would like to thank Ivy Fischer Stone and Fifi Oscard at Fifi Oscard Associates; Janet Schulman, Denise Cronin, and my editor, Regina Kahney, at Knopf; Marie Brown of Marie Brown Associates; Dr. Hank Murray; Concepcion Alvar; and Lynn Abraham, who all contributed greatly through their advice in the making of and the completion of this book.

Without the support and assistance of my friends, Lynn A., Linda B., Harriette M., Lee H., Toni P., Sheila F., Lee M., Jennifer L., Rhetta V., June G., Carole D., Brigitte L., Lisa C., Ariane C., and Machelle A., I would not have made it through these past eight months.

Most of all, my love and thanks go to Camera and to Arthur for their endurance, their love, and their example. It will always remain with me.

THIS IS A BORZOI BOOK PUBLISHED BY ALFRED A. KNOPF, INC.

Copyright © 1993 by Jeanne Moutoussamy-Ashe

All rights reserved under International and Pan-American Copyright Conventions. Published in the United States by Alfred A. Knopf, Inc., New York, and simultaneously in Canada by Random House of Canada Limited, Toronto. Distributed by Random House, Inc., New York. Book design by Edward Miller.

Library of Congress Cataloging-in-Publication Data

Moutoussamy-Ashe, Jeanne.
Daddy and Me : a photo story of Arthur Ashe and his daughter, Camera / photographs and words by Jeanne Moutoussamy-Ashe.
  p. cm.
SUMMARY: Text and photographs provide insight into the relationship of tennis great Arthur Ashe and his six-year-old daughter Camera, showing young children how families deal with AIDS.
ISBN 0-679-85096-1 (trade) — ISBN 0-679-95096-6 (lib. bdg.)
1. Ashe, Arthur—Juvenile literature. 2. Tennis players—United States—Biography—Juvenile literature.
3. Fathers and daughters— (Disease)—Juvenile literature. [1. Ashe, Arthur. 2. Tennis players.
3. Fathers and daughters. 4. AIDS (Disease).] I. Title.
GV994.A7M68 1993 796.342´092—dc20 [B] 93-11513

Manufactured in the United States of America 10 9 8 7 6 5 4 3 2 1

To Daddy with love

J.M.A.

C.E.A.

A Note from the Author

This is a story about two very special people—my husband, Arthur, and my daughter, Camera. I created this book because of what I learned from both of them.

In September of 1988, three months before Camera's second birthday, Arthur and I learned that he had contracted AIDS from a blood transfusion in 1983. At the time, the word AIDS meant nothing to Camera, but she began to live with her daddy's illness every day. She lived with the constant diarrhea, the fevers, the fatigue. She always knew when Daddy didn't feel well.

When Camera was five, we gave Daddy's illness a name—"Camera, Daddy has AIDS." We expected her to be confused, yet her response surprised us: "You mean," she said, "like when Daddy has diarrhea and doesn't feel very good?"

This is when I began to learn about AIDS from Camera. For her, Daddy having AIDS was like her having the chickenpox or a stomach virus. You don't feel good, and you just want someone to love you and take care of you. For Camera, AIDS was simply an illness—and like any other illness, it was to be treated with compassion and support.

Then one night Arthur and I were sitting at the kitchen table with Camera, talking about ways to describe what it means to have AIDS, particularly to Camera's friends. It occurred to us that it would be wonderful to write a book from Camera's point of view about how she and her daddy have lived with AIDS. We agreed that the best way to illustrate the book would be with photographs of Camera and

Arthur and words in Camera's own voice. We wanted to give other parents a way to discuss AIDS with their young children.

That is how *Daddy and Me* was conceived. But there were other reasons for creating this book. Arthur understood what it was like to lose a parent at an early age. His mother had died when he was six and a half years old. During his entire life, he longed for memories of her, and only one remained clear. It was the last time he saw her, in the doorway of his home, in 1950, as he left for school. She was dressed in a blue corduroy robe. Few photos and no moving images existed of her. How he longed to know what she felt like, what she smelled and tasted like, and how she moved. As hard as he tried, he could not conjure up those images.

After Camera was born, whenever a "photo opportunity" came up and I was not close by with my camera, Arthur and Camera would call out, "Take our picture, Mommy!" I did so, and often, with the intention of documenting the love that existed in this family.

What you will see here is a portrait of Arthur and Camera as they care for each other on bad days and play together as father and daughter on good days. What you will hear in Camera's own words is that love is the best medicine.

Arthur died on February 6, 1993, and left Camera and me with the most important lesson of all: the power of love is everlasting. I hope you will use this book to share that lesson with your own children.

Jeanne Moutoussamy-Ashe
New York City
August 1993

This is me. My name is Camera.

This is my daddy and his name is Arthur.
I have lots of fun with my daddy.

But sometimes Daddy gets sick because he has AIDS.
Do you know what having AIDS means? I do.

It means that sometimes Daddy runs a fever
and feels very tired.

Like when you have a stomach ache.
You just don't feel very good.

Daddy has some bad days and lots of good days.
On good days we go to the tennis court.

Daddy was a tennis champion.
Now, when he gives lessons,
I help him pick up the balls.

Sometimes Daddy takes me to
the park and I climb trees.

Or we sit in the sun and sing.

On Daddy's bad days, I take care
of him. I give him his pills.

I take his temperature.
I make him wait until the thermometer
beeps, just like he does for me.

I shake his bottle of medicine and turn on the machine that helps him breathe it in.

The machine goes *HUMMMM!* but I get used to it.

Then I do a good job holding the bottle, so that Daddy can do a good job breathing.

Daddy gives me a big kiss when I help him.
He says that makes him feel better too.

Daddy helps take care of me too.
He likes to wash my hair.

Then he
combs it out.

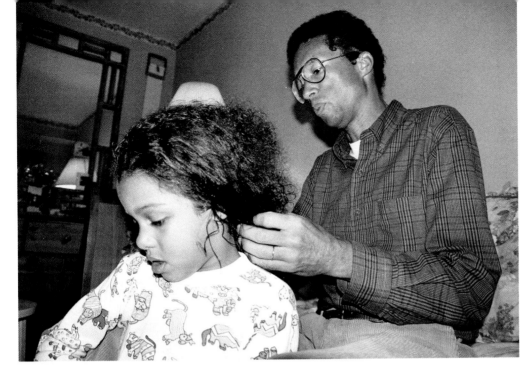

That is, if I sit still!

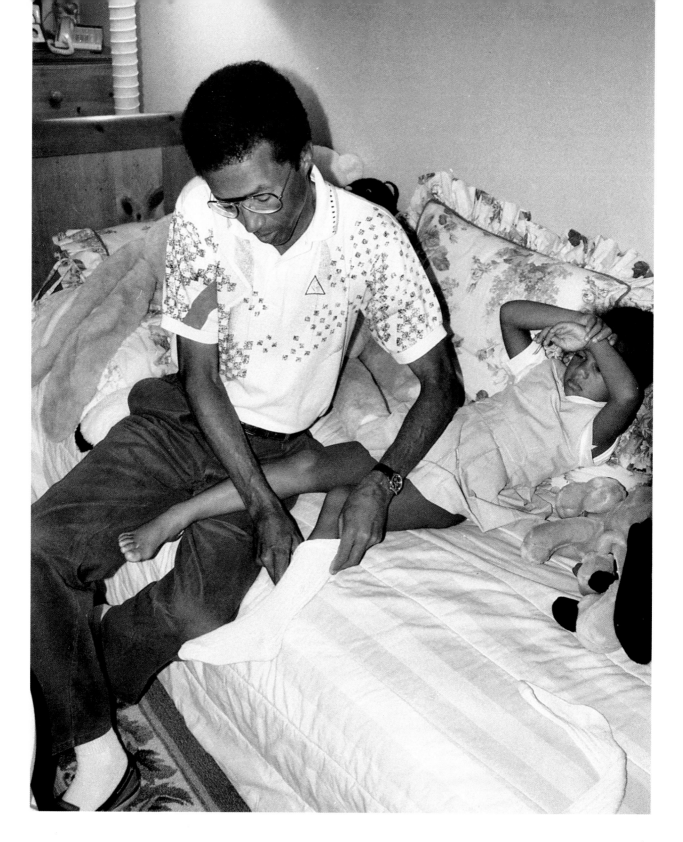

Daddy is my best buddy. In the mornings
he helps me get dressed for school.

At night he reads me two stories
before I go to sleep.
Sometimes he changes the words
to see if I am really listening.
But I catch him and it makes me laugh!

Some nights, when Daddy doesn't feel well, I read to *him!*
He is a good listener, and even turns the pages for me.

Then he tucks me in. But first we say our prayers.

God bless Mommy,
God bless Daddy,
God bless Camera,
God bless Crystal,
God bless Grandmother and Boompa,
God bless Grandma and Grandpa,
God bless Lizzie. . . .

I have good days and bad days too.
On my good days I like to hang upside down.

And I love to go to the gas station, because
Daddy lets me pump the gas. Fill 'er up!

On my bad days, when I'm sick and have to stay in, Daddy takes good care of me.

We sit and string beads together.
Daddy's favorite color is yellow. Mine is pink.

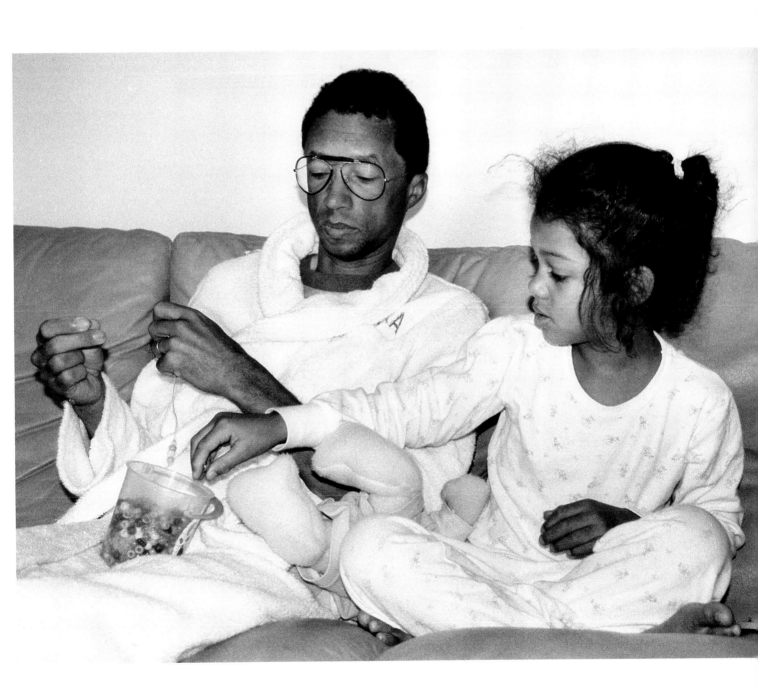

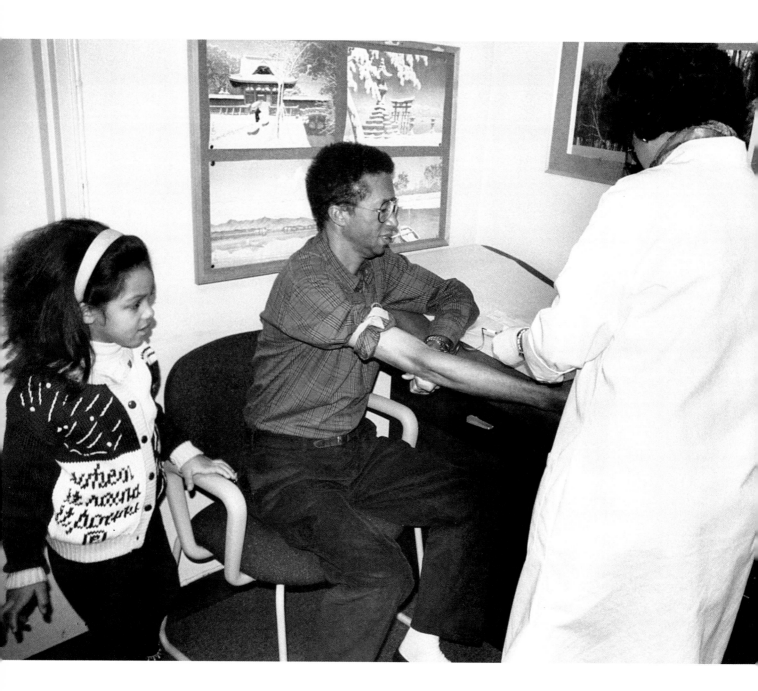

Every month, Daddy has to go to the hospital to get his blood tested and he takes me along.

Daddy is so brave when the nurse puts the needle in his arm.

One time Daddy had
to spend three weeks
in the hospital.
I went to visit him,
and we played with a
plastic model of
a heart.

Daddy taught me
where the heart is
inside your chest
and how it pumps
blood.

We took the model
apart and put it back
together, just like a
puzzle.

Peekaboo! I see you!

In the hospital, I listened to Daddy's heart, and he listened to mine.

Daddy got AIDS from a blood transfusion during a heart operation. A transfusion is when you transfer blood from one person to another. And Daddy got blood from a person who had AIDS.

Sometimes, when I visit Daddy in the hospital, we play too much and he gets tired. Then I sit and color while Daddy watches and rests.

When it's time to go home, I stick my hospital
pass on my forehead to make Daddy laugh.

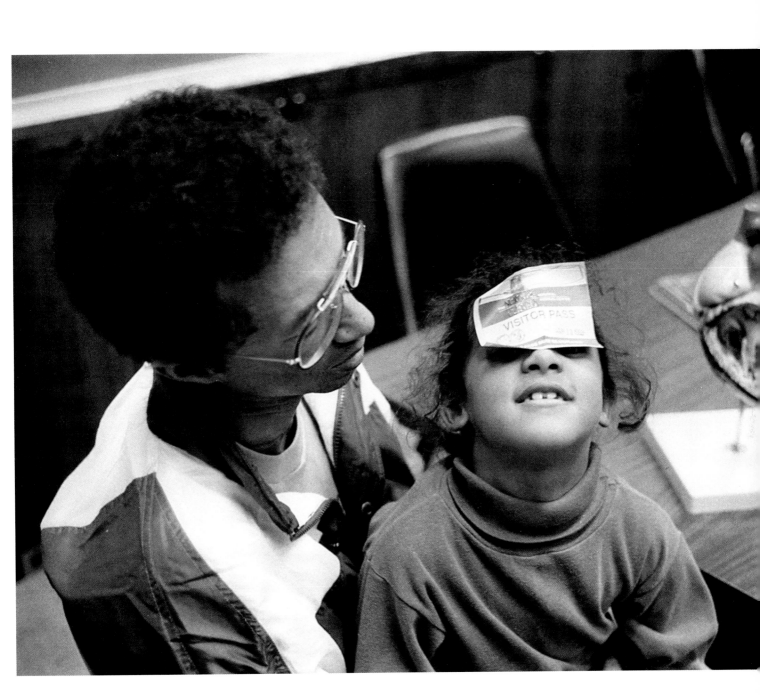

Then we play our favorite game:

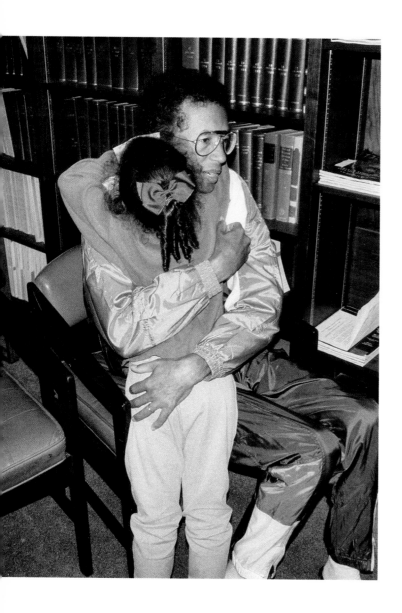 

BIG HUG   little hug

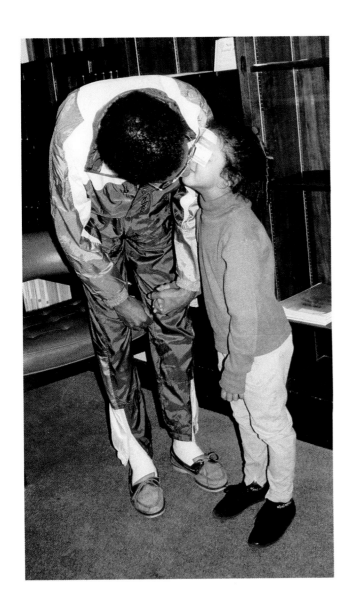

BIG KISS   little kiss

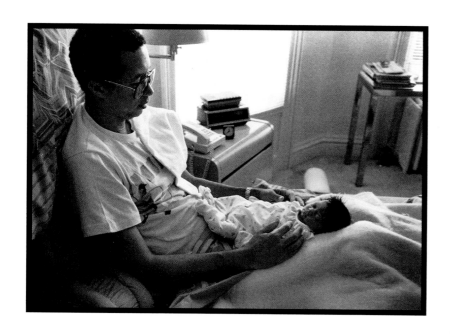

Ever since I was a baby,
Daddy loved to hold me.

I have learned lots of things from my daddy.
And one thing's for sure—I love my daddy and
my daddy loves me. That is the best medicine
and we both agree!

ARMENIA AUSTRALIA AUSTRIA AZERBAIJAN  BAHAMAS BAHRAIN BANGLADESH

 -HERZEGOVINA BOTSWANA BRAZIL  BRUNEI BULGARIA BURKINA FASO BURMA

 CHILE CHINA COLOMBIA COMOROS CONGO COSTA RICA CROATIA

 ECUADOR EGYPT EL SALVADOR EQUATORIAL GUINEA ERITREA ESTONIA

 GERMANY GHANA GREECE GREENLAND GRENADA GUATEMALA GUINEA

 INDIA INDONESIA IRAN IRAQ IRELAND ISRAEL ITALY

 KOREA, NORTH KOREA, SOUTH KUWAIT KYRGYZSTAN LAOS LATVIA LEBANON

 MACEDONIA MADAGASCAR MALAWI MALAYSIA MALDIVES MALI MALTA

 MOROCCO MOZAMBIQUE NAMIBIA NAURU NEPAL NETHERLANDS NEW ZEALAND

 PANAMA  PAPUA NEW GUINEA PARAGUAY PERU PHILIPPINES POLAND PORTUGAL

 SAUDI ARABIA SENEGAL SEYCHELLES SIERRA LEONE SINGAPORE SLOVAK REPUBLIC SLOVENIA

 ST VINCENT SUDAN  SURINAM SWAZILAND SWEDEN SWITZERLAND SYRIA

 TUNISIA TURKEY TURKMENISTAN TUVALU UGANDA  UKRAINE  UNITED ARAB EMIRATES

 VIETNAM WESTERN SAMOA YEMEN YUGOSLAVIA ZAÏRE ZAMBIA ZIMBABWE